Academic Encounters

2nd Edition

Bernard Seal
Series Editor: Bernard Seal

Human
Behavior 4

READING
——————
WRITING

CAMBRIDGE
UNIVERSITY PRESS

CAMBRIDGE UNIVERSITY PRESS
Cambridge, New York, Melbourne, Madrid, Cape Town,
Singapore, São Paulo, Delhi, Mexico City

Cambridge University Press
32 Avenue of the Americas, New York, NY 10013-2473, USA

www.cambridge.org
Information on this title: www.cambridge.org/9781107603004

First published 1997
Second edition 2012

Printed in Hong Kong, China, by Golden Cup Company Limited

A catalog record for this publication is available from the British Library.

ISBN 978-1-107-60297-7 Student's Book
ISBN 978-1-107-60300-4 Teacher's Manual

Additional resources for this publication at www.cambridge.org/academicencounters

Art direction, book design, and photo research: Integra
Layout services: Integra

Table of Contents

Scope & Sequence   4

Introduction   8

Student Book Answer Key   16

Content Quizzes   33

Content Quizzes Answer Key   41

Scope and sequence

Unit 1: Belonging to a Group • 1

	Content	**R** Reading Skills	**W** Writing Skills
Chapter 1 The Influence of Mind over Body page 4	**Reading 1** What Is Stress? **Reading 2** Coping with Stress **Reading 3** Stress and Illness	Thinking about the topic Predicting Reading for main ideas Thinking about what you already know Scanning Thinking critically	Parallel sentence structure Hedging
Chapter 2 Lifestyle and Health page 29	**Reading 1** Heart Disease **Reading 2** Smoking **Reading 3** Healthful Behavior	Personalizing the topic Skimming Thinking about the topic Increasing reading speed Comprehension after speed reading Scanning Thinking critically Scientific terms Reading for main ideas	Comparing Understanding paragraph structure

Unit 2: Gender in Society • 55

	Content	**R** Reading Skills	**W** Writing Skills
Chapter 3 The Teen Years page 58	**Reading 1** Defining Adolescence **Reading 2** Physical Change in Adolescence **Reading 3** Cognitive and Social Development in Adolescence	Personalizing the topic Previewing art Reading for main ideas Previewing art and graphics Skimming Reading for details Thinking critically	Understanding paragraph structure Understanding text structure Hedging Gerunds as subjects
Chapter 4 Adulthood page 82	**Reading 1** Early Adulthood **Reading 2** Middle Adulthood **Reading 3** Late Adulthood	Personalizing the topic Previewing art and graphics Reading actively Thinking about the topic Applying what you have read Examining graphics Increasing reading speed Comprehension after speed reading	Using data from a graphic Journal writing Paragraph topics Paragraph main ideas Supporting main ideas Paraphrasing

V Vocabulary Skills	**A** Academic Success Skills	Learning Outcomes
Guessing meaning from context Dealing with unknown words The Academic Word List	Highlighting Preparing for a test Answering multiple-choice questions Taking notes using arrows	Write an essay on health risk factors
Describing change Describing experimental results	Answering true/false questions Preparing for a short-answer test Writing short answers to test questions	

V Vocabulary Skills	**A** Academic Success Skills	Learning Outcomes
Word families Synonyms	Definition answers on tests The SQ3R System (Part 1) Taking notes in the margins The SQ3R System (Part 2)	Write an essay comparing and contrasting two adjacent periods of life
Collocations Guessing meaning from context Describing change	Synthesizing Group projects	

Unit 3: Media and Society • 109

	Content	R Reading Skills	W Writing Skills
Chapter 5 **Body Language** page 112	**Reading 1** Gestural Communication **Reading 2** Facial Communication **Reading 3** Eye Communication	Thinking about the topic Thinking of your own examples Thinking critically Skimming Personalizing the topic Increasing reading speed Comprehension after speed reading	Defining language Signaling examples Paraphrasing
Chapter 6 **Touch, Space, and Culture** page 137	**Reading 1** The Meanings of Touch **Reading 2** Spatial Messages **Reading 3** Nonverbal Communication and Culture	Thinking about the topic Skimming Reading for details Gathering data Predicting	The passive voice Summarizing Using adverbs Generalizations about groups of people Transitional expressions

Unit 4: Breaking the Rules • 163

	Content	R Reading Skills	W Writing Skills
Chapter 7 **Friendship** page 166	**Reading 1** What is Friendship? **Reading 2** The First Encounter **Reading 3** The Internet and Relationships	Thinking about the topic Predicting Personalizing the topic Previewing art Skimming Reading for details Increasing reading speed Comprehension after speed reading	Efficient sentence structure Understanding paragraph structure Journal writing Paraphrasing Summarizing
Chapter 8 **Love** page 190	**Reading 1** Attraction Theory **Reading 2** Love **Reading 3** Gender Differences in Loving	Personalizing the topic Reading for main ideas Reading for details Thinking about the topic Predicting Thinking critically	Journal writing Using quotations The passive voice

V Vocabulary Skills	A Academic Success Skills	Learning Outcomes
Words related to the topic Guessing meaning from context Ways of looking	Outlining practice Highlighting Taking notes Exploring key concepts Writing short answers to test questions	Produce a handbook that will help someone who is not a member of your culture understand how your culture uses body language
Word families Collocations	Making a chart Answering a short-answer test question Exploring key concepts Synthesizing	

V Vocabulary Skills	A Academic Success Skills	Learning Outcomes
Using new words in context Words related to the topic Collocations	Outlining practice Exploring key concepts	Write an essay in which you analyze one or two of your personal relationships
Prepositions Words related to the topic Similar and different	Mnemonics Preparing for a test Taking notes	

Introduction

The *Academic Encounters* Series

Academic Encounters is a sustained content-based series for English language learners preparing to study college-level subject matter in English. The goal of the series is to expose students to the types of texts and tasks that they will encounter in their academic course work and provide them with the skills to be successful when that encounter occurs.

At each level in the series, there are two thematically paired books. One is an academic reading and writing skills book, in which students encounter readings that are based on authentic academic texts. In this book, students are given the skills to understand texts and respond to them in writing. The reading and writing book is paired with an academic listening and speaking skills book, in which students encounter discussion and lecture material specially prepared by experts in their field. In this book, students learn how to take notes from a lecture, participate in discussions, and prepare short presentations.

The books at each level may be used as stand-alone reading and writing books or listening and speaking books. Or they may be used together to create a complete four-skills course. This is made possible because the content of each book at each level is very closely related. Each unit and chapter, for example, has the same title and deals with similar content, so that teachers can easily focus on different skills, but the same content, as they toggle from one book to the other. Additionally, if the books are taught together, when students are presented with the culminating unit writing or speaking assignment, they will have a rich and varied supply of reading and lecture material to draw on.

A sustained content-based approach

The *Academic Encounters* series adopts a sustained content-based approach, which means that at each level in the series students study subject matter from one or two related academic content areas. There are two major advantages gained by students who study with materials that adopt this approach.

- Because all the subject matter in each book is related to a particular academic discipline, concepts and language tend to recur. This has a major facilitating effect. As students progress through the course, what at first seemed challenging feels more and more accessible. Students thus gain confidence and begin to feel that academic study in English is not as overwhelming a task as they might at first have thought.

- The second major advantage in studying in a sustained content-based approach is that students actually gain some in-depth knowledge of a particular subject area. In other content-based series, in which units go from one academic discipline to another, students' knowledge of any one subject area is inevitably superficial. However, after studying a level of *Academic Encounters* students may feel that they have sufficiently good grounding in the subject area that they may decide to move on to study the academic subject area in a mainstream class, perhaps fulfilling one of their general education requirements.

The four levels in the series

The *Academic Encounters* series consists of four pairs of books designed for four levels of student proficiency. Each pair of books focuses on one or more related academic subject areas commonly taught in college-level courses.

- *Academic Encounters* 1: The Natural World
  Level 1 in the series focuses on earth science and biology. The books are designed for students at the low-intermediate level.

- *Academic Encounters* 2: American Studies
  Level 2 in the series focuses on American history, politics, government, and culture. The books are designed for students at the intermediate level.
- *Academic Encounters* 3: Life in Society
  Level 3 in the series focuses on sociological topics. The books are designed for students at the high-intermediate level.
- *Academic Encounters* 4: Human Behavior
  Level 4 in the series focuses on psychology and human communication. The books are designed for students at the low-advanced to advanced level.

New in the Second Edition

The second edition of the *Academic Encounters* series retains the major hallmark of the series: the sustained content approach with closely related pairs of books at each level. However, lessons learned over the years in which *Academic Encounters* has been on the market have been heeded in the publication of this brand new edition. As a result, the second edition marks many notable improvements that will make the series even more attractive to the teacher who wants to fully prepare his or her students to undertake academic studies in English.

New in the series

Four units, eight chapters per level. The number of units and chapters in each level has been reduced from five units / ten chapters in the first edition to four units / eight chapters in the second edition. This reduction in source material will enable instructors to more easily cover the material in each book.

Increased scaffolding. While the amount of reading and listening material that students have to engage with has been reduced, there has been an increase in the number of tasks that help students access the source material, including a greater number of tasks that focus on the linguistic features of the source material.

Academic Vocabulary. In both the reading and writing and the listening and speaking books, there are tasks that now draw students' attention to the academic vocabulary that is embedded in the readings and lectures, including a focus on the Academic Word list (AWL). All the AWL words encountered during the readings and lectures are also listed in an appendix at the back of each book.

Full color new design. A number of features have been added to the design, not only to make the series more attractive, but more importantly to make the material easier to navigate. Each task is coded so that teachers and students can see at a glance what skill is being developed. In addition, the end-of-unit writing skill and speaking skill sections are set off in colored pages that make them easy to find.

New in the reading and writing books

More writing skill development. In the first edition of *Academic Encounters*, the reading and writing books focused primarily on reading skills. In the second edition, the two skills are much more evenly weighted, making these books truly reading and writing books.

End-of-chapter and unit writing assignments. At the end of each chapter and unit, students are taught about aspects of academic writing and given writing assignments. Step-by step scaffolding is provided in these sections to ensure that students draw on the content, skills, and language they studied in the unit; and can successfully complete the assignments.

New and updated readings. Because many of the readings in the series are drawn from actual discipline-specific academic textbooks, recent editions of those textbooks have been used to update and replace readings.

New in the listening and speaking books

More speaking skill development. In the first edition of *Academic Encounters*, the listening and speaking books focused primarily on listening skills. In the second edition, the two skills in each of the books are more evenly weighted.

End-of-unit assignments. Each unit concludes with a review of the academic vocabulary introduced in the unit, a topic review designed to elicit the new vocabulary, and an oral presentation related to the unit topics, which includes step-by-step guidelines in researching, preparing, and giving different types of oral presentations.

New and updated lectures and interviews. Because the material presented in the interviews and lectures often deals with current issues, some material has been updated or replaced to keep it interesting and relevant for today's students.

Video of the lectures. In addition to audio CDs that contain all the listening material in the listening and speaking books, the series now contains video material showing the lectures being delivered. These lectures are on DVD and are packaged in the back of the *Student Books*.

The *Academic Encounters* Reading and Writing Books

Skills

There are two main goals of the *Academic Encounters* reading and writing books. The first is to give students the skills and confidence to approach an academic text, read it efficiently and critically, and take notes that extract the main ideas and key details. The second is to enable students to display the knowledge that has been gained from the reading either in a writing assignment or in a test-taking situation.

To this end, tasks in the *Academic Encounters* reading and writing books are color-coded and labeled as R **R** *Reading Skill* tasks, V **V** *Vocabulary Skill* tasks, W **W** *Writing Skill* tasks, and A **A** *Academic Success* tasks. At the beginning of each unit, all the skills taught in the unit are listed in a chart for easy reference.

- **Reading Skills R**. The reading skill tasks are designed to help students develop strategies before reading, while reading, and after reading. The pre-reading tasks, such as Skimming for Main Ideas, teach students strategies they can employ to facilitate their first reading of a text. Post-reading tasks, such as *Identifying Main Ideas* and *Reading Critically* give students the tools to gain the deepest understanding possible of the text.
- **Vocabulary Skills V**. Vocabulary learning is an essential part of improving one's ability to read an academic text. Many tasks throughout the books focus on particular sets of vocabulary that are important for reading in a particular subject area as well as the sub-technical vocabulary that is important for reading in any academic discipline. At the end of each chapter, some of the AWL words that appeared in the readings of the chapter are listed and an exercise is given that checks students' knowledge of those words.
- **Writing Skills W**. There are two types of writing skills throughout the books. One type might more accurately be described as reading-for-writing skills in that students are asked to notice features of the texts that they have been reading in order to gain insight into how writers construct text. The other type is writing development skills, and these appear in the mid-unit and end-of-unit writing sections and overtly instruct students how to write academic texts, in which main ideas are supported with examples and in which plagiarism is avoided.
- **Academic Success A**. Besides learning how to read, write, and build their language proficiency, students also have to learn other skills that are particularly important in academic settings. These include such skills as learning how to prepare for a content test, answer certain types of test questions, take notes, and work in study groups. *Academic Encounters* makes sure that this important dimension of being a student in which English is the medium of instruction is not ignored.

Readings

There are three readings in each chapter of the *Academic Encounters* reading and writing books. Readings vary in length and difficulty depending on the level of the book. The readings in the upper two levels contain texts that in many cases are unchanged from the college textbooks from which they were taken. The readings in the two lower-level books make use of authentic source materials. They are adapted so that they can be better processed by lower-level students, but great pains have been taken to retain the authentic flavor of the original materials.

Tasks

Before and after each reading, students are given tasks that activate one or more of the target skills in the book. The first time a task is introduced in the book, it is accompanied by a colored commentary box that explains which skill is being practiced and why it is important. When the task type occurs again later in the book, it is sometimes accompanied by another commentary box, as a reminder or to present new information about the skill. At the back of the book, there is an alphabetized index of all the skills covered in the tasks.

Order of units

In each book, a rationale exists for the order of the unit topics. Teachers may choose a different order if they wish; however, because reading skills and writing skills are developed sequentially throughout the books, teaching the units in the order that they occur is optimal. If teachers do choose to teach the units out of order, they can refer to the Skills Index at the back of the book to see what types of tasks have been presented in earlier units and build information from those tasks into their lessons.

Course length

Each unit in the *Academic Encounters* reading and writing books will take approximately 20 hours to teach. The six readings per unit should take about two to two and a half hours to teach, with about twenty minutes to be spent on the pre-reading activities. The two academic writing development sections can be taught as two writing workshops, each taking roughly two to two and a half hours to teach.

The course can be made shorter or longer. To shorten the course, teachers might choose not to do every task in the book and to assign some tasks and texts as homework, rather than do them in class. To lengthen the course, teachers might choose to supplement the book with content-related material from their own files, to assign Internet research, and to spend more time on the writing assignments.

Unit Content Quizzes

The *Academic Encounters* series adopts a sustained content-based approach in which students experience what it is like to study an academic discipline in an English-medium instruction environment. In such classes, students are held accountable for learning the content of the course by the administering of tests.

In the *Academic Encounters* series, we also believe that students should go back and study the content of the book and prepare for a test. This review of the material in the books simulates the college learning experience, and makes students review the language and content that they have studied.

At the back of this *Teacher's Manual* are four reproducible content quizzes, one for each unit in the book. Each quiz contains a mixture of true/false questions, multiple choice, and short-answer questions, plus one question that requires a longer one- or two-paragraph answer. The tests should take about 50 minutes of class time. Students should be given time to prepare for the test, but should take it as soon as possible after completing the unit.

General Teaching Guidelines

In this section, we give some very general instructions for teaching the following elements that occur in each unit of the *Academic Encounters* listening and speaking books:

- The unit opener, which contains a preview of the unit content, skills, and learning outcomes
- The *Preparing to Read* sections, which occur before each reading
- The *Readings*, which are sometimes accompanied by short boxed readings
- The *After You Read* sections, which follow each reading
- The *Academic Vocabulary Review* sections, which are at the end of each chapter
- The *Developing Writing Skills* sections, which are at the end of the first chapter of each unit
- The *Practice Academic Writing* sections, which occur at the end of the second chapter of each unit

Unit Opener

The opening page of the unit contains the title of the unit, a photograph that is suggestive of the content of the unit, and a brief paragraph that summarizes the unit. Make sure that students understand what the title means. Have them look at the art on the page and describe it and talk about how it might relate to the title.

Finally look at the summary paragraph at the bottom of the page. Read it with your students and check to be sure that they understand the vocabulary and key concepts. At this point it is not necessary to introduce the unit topics in any depth, since they will get a detailed preview of the contents of the unit on the third page of the unit.

On the second page of the unit, students can preview the chapter and reading titles and see what skills are being taught throughout the unit. Have students read and understand the chapter and reading titles, and then focus on a few of the skills listed. Note those that students might already be familiar with and some new ones that are being taught for the first time in the book. Draw students' attention to the *Learning Outcomes* at the bottom of the page. This alerts students to what they are expected to be able to do by the end of the unit. It is also essentially a preview of the major assignment of the unit.

On the third page of the unit are tasks that preview the unit either by having students predict what information they might find in each section of the unit or by giving them some information from the unit and having them respond to it. The first couple of times that you teach from this page, tell students that when they are given a longer reading assignment, such as a chapter of a textbook, it is always a good strategy for them to preview the titles and headings of the reading, predict what the reading might be about, and to think about what they might already know about the subject matter.

The unit opener section should take about an hour of class time.

Preparing to Read

Each reading is preceded by a page of pre-reading tasks in a section called Preparing to Read. Pre-reading is heavily emphasized in the *Academic Encounters* reading and writing books since it is regarded as a crucial step in the reading process. Some pre-reading activities introduce students to new vocabulary; some teach students to get an overall idea of the content by surveying the text for headings, graphic material, captions, and art, and others have students recall their prior knowledge of the topic and their personal experiences to help them assimilate the material that they are about to encounter in the reading.

Although one or two pre-reading tasks are always included for each text, you should look for ways to supplement these tasks with additional pre-reading activities. As you and your students work your way through the book, students will become exposed to more and more pre-reading strategies. Having been exposed to these, students should be adding them to their repertoire, and you should encourage their regular use. For example, after having practiced the skill of examining graphic material, previewing headings and subheadings, and skimming for main ideas, students should ideally carry out these operations every time they approach a new reading.

As a general principle, the lower the proficiency level of the students, the greater is the need to spend time on the pre-reading activities. The more pre-reading tasks students undertake, the easier it is for students to access the text when it comes time for them to do a close reading.

Each *Preparing to Read* page should take about thirty minutes of class time. Some may require more or less time.

Reading

Once it comes time for students to read the text, how closely should they do so at this point? Some students believe that after doing the *Preparing to Read* tasks, they should now read the text slowly and carefully. They will be particularly tempted to do so because the texts have been crafted to be intentionally challenging for them, since students need to be prepared to read challenging, authentic, un-simplified text in their academic studies. However, students should be discouraged from doing this. For one thing, it is a poor use of class time to have students poring silently over a text for 20 minutes or more. More importantly, it is vital that students train themselves to read quickly, tolerating some ambiguity and going for understanding the main ideas and overall text structure, rather than every word and detail.

To promote faster reading, the book includes one Increasing *Reading Speed* task per unit. In this task, students are encouraged to read the text as quickly as possible, using techniques that can help them read faster while retaining a fairly high level of comprehension. If students consistently apply these techniques, most texts will take between 3 and 7 minutes to read. Before students start reading any text, therefore, it is a good idea to give them a challenging time limit, which they should aim toward to complete their reading of the text.

An alternative to reading every text in class is to assign some of the longer texts as homework. When you do this, you should do the pre-reading tasks in class at the end of the lesson and start the next class by having students quickly skim the text again before moving on to the *After You Read* tasks.

After You Read

Sometimes, after students have completed reading the text, the first order of business is not to move on to the *After You Read* tasks, but to revisit the Preparing to Read tasks to check to see if students had the correct answers in a predicting or skimming activity.

The tasks in the *After You Read* section are varied. Some focus on the content of the reading, some on the linguistic features of the reading, such as the vocabulary and grammar, and some on the organization of the text. There are also tasks that teach study skills. No two *After You Read* sections are the same (in fact, no two *After You Read* tasks are quite the same) because the content, organization, and the language of the reading dictate the types of tasks that would be appropriate.

Teachers who are used to more conventional post-reading tasks may be surprised to find that the focus of the post-reading is not text comprehension. This is because the intention of every task in the *Academic Encounters* reading and writing books is to develop a skill, not to test comprehension.

The following are the main functions of the post-reading activities in the *Academic Encounters* reading and writing books:

- to have students read for main ideas and think critically about the text
- to ask students to think about the content of the text, find a personal connection to it, or apply new information learned from the text in some way
- to highlight some of the most salient language in the text, either vocabulary or grammatical structures, and have students use that language in some way
- to have students gain insight into the style and organization of the text and to use those insights to help them become more effective writers themselves
- to develop students' repertoire of study skills by teaching them, for example, how to highlight a text, take notes, and summarize
- to develop students' test-preparation skills by familiarizing them with certain question types and by asking them to assess what they would need to do if they were going to be tested on the text.

To make the course as lively as possible, student interaction has been built into most activities. Thus, although the books are primarily intended to build reading and writing skills, opportunities for speaking abound. Students discuss the content of the texts, they work collaboratively to solve task problems, they compare answers in pairs or small groups, and sometimes they engage in role-playing.

Academic Vocabulary Review

The final exercise of each chapter lists words from the Academic Word List that students encountered in the chapter readings. The first time that you do this exercise, discuss the meaning of "academic word." Tell students that it is a word that occurs frequently across all types of academic texts regardless of the academic subject matter. As such, these are words that deserve students' special attention. Encourage students to learn these words and point out that at the back of the book there is an appendix of words from the Academic Word List that occurred in the readings. Promote the value of learning words from this appendix during their study of the course.

Developing Writing Skills

The *Developing Writing Skills* section of the unit occurs in the middle of the unit between the two chapters. In this section, students learn about some aspect of the writing process, such as how to write topic sentences, how to organize a paragraph or an essay, how to summarize, and how to avoid plagiarism. In the *Academic Encounters* reading and writing books Levels 1-2, the focus is primarily on learning how to write paragraphs. In the higher two levels, 3-4, the focus is on longer pieces of text, including academic essays.

In the first part of the section, the particular sub-skill that is the focus of the section is presented in an information box with clear examples. In the second part of the section, students are given a number of discrete activities to practice these writing sub-skills. Many of the activities in this section are collaborative. Teachers might therefore want to set up a writing workshop-style classroom when working on these sections, putting the students to work in pairs or small groups and circulating among them, checking on their progress and giving individualized feedback.

Practice Academic Writing

The two sections of the unit that are devoted entirely to writing instruction are both set off on lightly-colored pages so that teachers can easily locate them throughout the book. This enables teachers or students to use them as reference sections and come back to them frequently as they work their way through the book.

The second writing section, *Practice Academic Writing*, occurs at the very end of the unit. In this section, students are given a writing assignment and guided through steps in the writing process to help them satisfactorily complete the assignment. The writing assignments draw from content from the unit, so students are asked to go back to the readings in order to complete the assignments. In addition, students are reminded of any linguistic features that were the focus of instruction in the unit and are prompted to attempt to use such language in their own writing.

The *Practice Academic Writing* section is divided into three parts: Preparing to Write, Now Write, and After You Write. In these three parts, students do pre-writing work (Preparing to Write), write a first draft (Now Write), and revise and edit their work (After You Write).

The *Practice Academic Writing* section may well stretch over two or more class periods, with teachers varying the amount of in-class and out-of-class time spent on writing. The Preparing to Write part should be done in class. Here the students are presented with the assignment and are given some pre-writing activities that will aid them in writing their first draft. The *Now Write* part should at least sometimes be done in class so that teachers can accurately assess the strength of a student's writing.

It is recommended that teachers go through the *After You Write* part of the section in a different class from the first two parts of this section, so that they have a chance to provide feedback on students' writing and students have a chance to digest and apply that feedback. Remind students that good writers almost always write and re-write their texts several times and that the more re-writing of their texts that they do, the better writers they will eventually become.

Chapter 1
The Influence of Mind over Body

Reading 1 – What Is Stress?

After You Read

1 Highlighting Page 7
B

- stressor - stimuli or events in our environment that make physical and emotional demands on us:
  stress - our emotional and physical reactions to such stimuli
- what all stressors have in common: they interfere with or threaten our accustomed way of life
- Stage 1: the person or animal first becomes aware of the stressor
- Stage 2: the organism becomes highly alert and aroused, energized by a burst of epinephrine
- Stage 3: the organism tries to adapt to the stressful stimulus or to escape from it.
- Main idea sentence: Whether a particular stimulus will be stressful depends on the person's subjective appraisal of that stimulus.

2 Preparing for a test Page 7

1. A stressor is a stimulus or event in the environment which brings on stress.
2. The three stages of the general adaptation syndrome are: alarm reaction, resistance, exhaustion.
3. They both represent changes to our normal routine.
4. Whereas with rats we can always predict reactions to particular stressors, we cannot predict the reaction of humans. This is because what may be stressful to one person may not be stressful to another.

3 Guessing meaning from context Pages 8–9
Possible responses:
A

1. a hurricane or a tornado: very bad, harmful, or destructive events
2. daily hassles: small problems that bother us every day
3. in common: the same
4. accustomed: routine

B

collectively: together
alert and aroused: awake, aware, paying attention
epinephrine: a chemical that gives one more energy
subjective appraisal: personal feelings
threatening: dangerous
handled: was able to cope with or face
being called on: picked, selected
pounding: beating, pumping

4 Parallel sentence structure Page 9
A

1. … and sometimes it is applied to …
2. For another person, being called on to give a talk….
   …some give rise to anger, and some give rise to helplessness and depression.

B

Possible response:

Some stressors, such as losing a job, produce negative physical and emotional reactions, such as exhaustion and depression. Other stressors, like getting a new job or planning a vacation, give us energy and excitement.

Reading 2 – Coping with Stress

Preparing to Read

Predicting Page 11
B

1. b   2. b   3. b   4. b   5. a

After You Read

1 Reading for main ideas Page 15
A

c.

B

| a. Degree of control | b. Personality factors | c. Predictability |

C

1. b   2. a   3. c   4. c   5. c

D

Possible response:

According to research, there appear to be three main ways to cope with stress. First, you need to try to take some control of the stressful situation. For example, experiments with rats show that rats that can control a stressful event get fewer ulcers than rats that cannot control the event. Second, if you can predict that a stressful event is going to happen, you can cope with the event more easily. Thus, students prefer scheduled quizzes to surprise quizzes. Finally, you need to see a stressful event as a challenge, not a threat, and develop a stress resistant personality.

3 Answering multiple-choice questions Page 17

1. b   2. a   3. a   4. c

Reading 3 – Stress and Illness

Preparing to Read

2 Scanning Page 18

1. **Illnesses**: colds, cancer, arthritis, asthma, migraine headaches, ulcers.
2. **Jobs**: assembly-line workers, air-traffic controllers.
3. **Field of research**: Psychoimmunology
4. **Researcher**: Richard Shekelle
5. **Other names for PTSD**: shell shock, battle fatigue

After You Read

1 Taking notes using arrows Page 22
A

2. Stress reactions ↓immune system ↑ illnesses
3. Stress → ↑ hydorochloric acid in stomach → ↓ stomach lining → ulcers
4. ↑ Ulcers in workers in jobs ↑ psychological demands
5. prolonged stress → ↑ corticosteroids and ↓ norephinephrine → ↓ ability to fight cancer
6. depressed people ↑ drinking and smoking → ↑ cancer
7. widowed men ↓ white blood cell function

2 Hedging Page 23
A

1. many, can
2. seems to
3. can, at least in part
4. seem to suggest, may
5. tend to
6. There is also some evidence
7. can, can, might

3 Thinking critically Page 24
A

The following items are true according to the text: 1, 4, 5, 7, 8, 9

4 The Academic Word List Page 25
A

1. h	2. d	3. a	4. g	5. c
6. b	7. e	8. j	9. f	10. i

B

Stress comes about when a <u>major</u> change takes place in a person's life. <u>Data</u> from research suggest that when the <u>duration</u> of the stress is long, and the stress is <u>encountered</u> continually, then the chance of developing an illness is high. Several experiments have <u>demonstrated</u> that the immune system reacts to stress. This reaction <u>apparently</u> causes a <u>decline</u> in the immune system's effectiveness. However, there are also indications that the effects of stress can be <u>minimized</u> if people react to stress in an active way.

Chapter 1 Academic Vocabulary Review

Page 26

1. anticipate	7. schedule
2. conduct	8. collapse
3. expose	9. link
4. apparently	10. vary
5. consequences	11. beneficial
6. encounter	12. adapt

Chapter 2
Lifestyle and Health

Reading 1 – Heart Disease

Preparing to Read

2 Skimming Page 29

<u>2</u> 1.   6 2.   3 3.   1 4.   4 5.   5 6.

After You Read

1 Answering true/false
questions Page 33

1. T   6. F
2. F   7. F
3. T   8. T
4. T   9. F
5. F   10. T

2 Comparing Page 34
A

2. **competitive**
Type A people are more <u>competitive</u> than Type B people.
Type B people are less <u>competitive</u> than Type A people.
(or Type B people are not as competitive as Type A
People.)

3. **laid back**
Type B people are more laid back than Type A people.
Type A people are less aggressive than Type B people.
(or Type A people are not as laid back as Type B people.)

4. **good at controlling their emotions**
Type B people are better at controlling their emotions
than Type A people.
Type A people are worse at controlling their emotions
than Type B people.
(or Type A people are not as good at controlling their
emotions as Type B people.)

5. **achievement-oriented**
Type A people are more achievement-oriented than
Type B people.
Type B people are less achievement-oriented than
Type A people.
(or Type B people are not as achievement-oriented as
Type A people.)

6. **calm**
Type B people are calmer than Type A people.
Type A people are less calm than Type B people.
(or Type A people are not as calm as Type B people.)

B
Sample answers:
2. Type A people have a higher risk of having high blood
   pressure than Type B people.
3. Type A people have a higher rate of heart disease than
   Type B people.
4. Type A people have a greater sense of time urgency
   than Type B people.
5. Type B people have a calmer reaction to difficult
   situations than Type A people.

Reading 2 – Smoking

After You Read

1 Comprehension after speed
reading Pages 39–40

1. c   6. a
2. c   7. b
3. a   8. b
4. a   9. b
5. b   10. a

2 Scanning Page 40

1. 10 million
2. 35%
3. Florida
4. the early 1950s
5. America, Canada, and Britain
6. Japan
7. 70%
8. 1964
9. 50%

3 Describing change Page 41
A

↑	↓
grow to	reduce
soar	drop
increase	decline
raise	go down
skyrocket	
go up	

B

1. went up
2. reduced
3. soared
4. declined
5. skyrocketed
6. has dropped
7. increase
8. has declined
9. go down

Reading 3 – Healthful Behavior

Preparing to Read

2 Scientific terms Page 43

A

1. This refers to putting students into groups completely by chance, for example, by flipping a coin or pulling names out of a hat
2. In the case of this experiment, the control group is the students who do nothing different in their lives. They do neither the exercise nor the relaxation programs, which are the treatments – the aspect of their lives which is different and newly introduced for the experiment.
3. They were testing whether exercise or relaxation reduces the degree of depression among the subjects.

B

1. Researchers followed over 21 thousand people for 8 years. They found that those people who did not attend religious services were almost twice as likely to die younger than those who frequently attended religious services.
2. Not attending religious services (factor) correlated highly (1.87 more likely) with having died. Researches took into account (controlled for) age, sex, race, and religion (variables). They probably did this by matching up people of the same age, sex, etc, before comparing the death rates.

After You Read

1 Reading for main ideas Page 47

1. Exercise seems to make people not only physically healthier, but also emotionally healthier.
6. Exercising regularly can help you live a longer life and have fewer illnesses.

2 Understanding paragraph structure Page 47

Sample answers:

B

Possible explanations why religious involvement→ ↑ longevity

1. More women are religious and women outlive men
2. Religious people ↓ smoke and drink
3. Social support ↑
4. Divorce ↓

C

Researchers are now wondering why religious involvement increases longevity.

D

Consider one obvious possibility: exercise releases certain chemicals
Second, exercise may lead to sound sleep …
Third, people who exercise feel a sense of accomplishment.
Finally, one's improved physique may influence one's emotional state and …

3 Describing experimental results Page 48

1. *Suggests* means it may be true; shows means there is strong evidence that it is true.
2. *Shows* tells us that the experiment found something out for the first time; *confirms* tells us that a previous experiment or experiments yielded certain results and this latest experiment has the same results again.
3. We do not know. If we read further into the study, the research may tell us whether the study did, in fact, *succeed in correlating* the two things.
4. *Studies* are the experiments; *findings* are what the results of those experiments can tell us.
5. *Indicates* is stronger: *Suggests* means that the data may tell us something whereas *indicates*, while not 100% certain, means that the researcher has much more certainty about what the data tell us.
6. *Shows* is stronger: *Shows* means that the meaning of the results is clear whereas *indicates* tells us that we can accept the conclusion with a high degree of probability, but not certainty.
7. reveals that

4 Preparing for a short-answer test Page 49

A

Possible Answers:

Type 1

What are three benefits of exercise according to this reading?

How many more years on average would a person live who at age 20 was a frequent attendee at religious services, compared to someone who did not frequently attend religious services?

Describe the experiment involving mildly depressed female college students.

Type 2

What are differences in the behaviors of religious service attendees and religious service non-attendees that might explain why one group tends to live longer than the other?

Type 3 questions:

Evaluate the benefits of exercise compared to the benefits of spirituality. Which do you think might lead to a longer and healthier life?

5 Writing short answers to test questions Page 49

Answers will vary depending on Task 4 questions.

Chapter 2 Academic Vocabulary Review

Page 49

1. target
2. randomly
3. network
4. acknowledge
5. ambiguity
6. consumption
7. undergo
8. alter
9. odds
10. intense
11. coherent
12. considerably

Chapter 3
The Teen Years

Reading 1 – Defining Adolescence

After You Read

2 Understanding paragraph structure Page 61

1. biological, psychological, social
2. a. Sentences 1,2
   b. Sentences 3,4
   c. Sentences 5,6,7
3. a. Or
   b. Additionally
4. a. When adolescence is viewed in biological terms
   b. When adolescence is viewed from a psychological perspective
   c. Looking at adolescence as a social stage
5. There is no topic sentence. Two possible topic sentences might be: "There are three ways to define adolescence," or "Adolescence may be viewed from three very different perspectives."

4 Word families Page 62
A

1. specify   v
2. commitments   n
3. emphasizes   v
4. maturity   n
5. uncooperative   adj
6. negativism   n

Reading 2 – Physical Change in Adolescence

Preparing to Read

1 Previewing art and graphics Page 63

Sample Answers:

1. Girls start their growth spurt earlier than boys.
2. Girls stop growing earlier than boys.
3. Boys grow taller than girls

2 Skimming Page 63
A

a. 4   b. 5   c. 3   d. 2

After You Read

1 Reading for details Page 66
A

An early-blooming girl:
   could be "boy crazy"
   might marry younger than most
   might start dating younger than most
A late-blooming girl:
   can have time to develop broad interests
An early-blooming boy:
   might start dating younger than most
   is likely to have respect from peers
A late-blooming boy:
   may feel inadequate as an adult

B

a. 2   b. 3   c. 1   d. 4

2 Understanding text structure Page 66

Possible responses:

1. The introduction tells us that the reading will discuss physical changes in adolescence and how they can psychologically affect an individual. It also introduces the reader to the concept that the age a person hits puberty and the sex of the individual can also affect the impacts of puberty.

   Words/phrases: adolescence, biological and physical changes, growth spurt, psychological well-being, whether one is a boy or girl, very early or very late age.

2. The thesis statement is in the middle of the introduction: "Undergoing these changes may have a significant impact on an individual's psychological well-being."

   The thesis statement prepares the reader for the body paragraphs - Par 2: the physical changes of the growth spurt; Par 3: the psychological impact of physical changes in general; Par 4: affect of change on early and late bloomers; Par 5: focus on affect on late bloomers.

3. Yes, it summarizes that there are many changes that occur during adolescence.

3 Hedging Page 67
A

Paragraph 1: is **generally** marked by, **can** have an impact
Paragraph 2: **usually** occurs, **generally** show, **usually** don't reach, **generally** attain,
Paragraph 3: **at least some**, **may** be a direct result, it **is not uncommon**, **may** appear, **seldom**, **may** suffer
Paragraph 4: **many** boys and girls, will **probably**, **likely** to start
Paragraph 5: **there is some evidence**, **some** broadening interests, we **may** suggest, **may** suffer

C

Modals: can, may
Phrases: at least some, it is not uncommon, there is some evidence, it is likely
Adverbs: usually, generally, probably, seldom
Quantifiers: many, some,

4 Gerunds as subjects Page 67
A

2. Subject: Undergoing these changes at either a very early age or at a very late age compared to one's peers
Main verb: can have
3. Subject: Reaching puberty well before or well after others of one's age
Main verb: does have
4. Subject: ... being a late bloomer
Main verb: is

B

Answers will vary.

Reading 3 – Cognitive and Social Development in Adolescence
After You Read

3 Synonyms Pages 76–77

1. ponder – think about
2. contemplation of one's self – self analysis
3. trying things out – experiment
4. come to grips with – struggle
5. performing – "on stage"
6. unrealistic cognition – irrational beliefs
7. autonomy – independence
8. consult with the teenager – involve the teenager in decision making

Chapter 3 Academic Vocabulary Review

Page 78

1. period
2. conflict
3. constantly
4. perspective
5. status
6. theorist
7. approximately
8. resolve
9. undergo
10. transition
11. hence
12. evidence

Developing Writing Skills
Paraphrasing Pages 80–81
C

Paraphrase 3 is the best answer. It restructures the text, changes word order, replaces both words and phrases with synonymous words and phrases.

Chapter 4
Adulthood

Reading 1 – Early Adulthood

Preparing to Read

2 Previewing art and graphics Page 82
A

1. The medium age of men and women in the U.S. when they first married
2. *Answers will vary.*
3. *Answers will vary.*
4. *Answers will vary.*

After You Read

1 Reading actively Page 87

Possible answers:

1. At 18: marriage, the military, smoking, signing contracts. At 21: drinking, gambling
2. Boyfriend or girlfriend, husband or wife, perhaps young children, in-laws, new neighbors and community members, new co-workers, business connections, boss.
3. Trying to find the right person to be their husband or wife. Dating different people until they find the right one. For work, working at different places until they find the job that suits them best.
4. Socializing, going out, seeing friends. Negative consequences – less sleep, interrupted sleep, less time for oneself, less time alone with one's spouse, few opportunities to go out or vacation with one's spouse.
5. The joy of having a child, watching the child grow and reach stages of development – learning to talk, walk, read, begin and graduate from school, etc. Giving the child love and receiving love in return.
6. We are potentially at our strongest, quickest, and most agile. Our physical and mental capacities are at their peak. Our skin, eyesight, and flexibility are at their best.

2 Collocations Pages 87–88

1. a period
2. support
3. a choice
4. a career
5. possibilities
6. money
7. a path
8. a relationship
9. responsibilities
10. a family

3 Using data from a graphic Pages 88–89
A

1. c. 1   d. 2   a. 3   b. 4
2. & 3.

Figure 00 shows the median age at which men and women in the United States first got married between 1970 and 2008. | As can be seen, every year between 1970 and 2008 the median age of first marriage for both men and women went up. | For example, for men, it went up by 4.8 years, from 23.2 in 1970 to 28.0 in 2008. | For women, it went up by 5.4 years. In 1970, the median age at first marriage for women was just over twenty years of age, but by 2008 age the median age was 26.2 years. | One possible explanation for these data is that following the female liberation movement of the 1960s, women were looking to get more education, get better jobs, and become more independent.

Reading 3 – Middle Adulthood

Preparing to Read

2 Guessing meaning from context Page 90

1. transition – change
2. contemplate – think about
3. mortality – death
4. middle-age spread – bigger waistline
5. facial wrinkles – lines on the face
6. graying– getting gray
7. sensory capacities – hearing, sight, etc
8. diminish – decrease, worsen

After You Read

1 Paragraph topics Page 93
3   5   6   2   7   4   1

2 Paragraph main ideas Page 93
A
6   7   3   1   2

B

Possible responses:

The physical changes that begin in middle adulthood remind us of our mortality.

Midlife crisis is real for both men and women, although they may respond to it differently.

3 Supporting main ideas Page 94

Possible responses:

A

Main idea: The midlife crisis is more of a stereotype than a reality.

1. Divorce is more common among those in their 20's
2. Suicide is more common among those in their 70's
3. There is no peak in distress during the midlife years
4. They report that it is another event such as illness or job loss rather than age that creates the crisis.

B

Main idea: The mid-life crisis is a stereotype.

Support 1: Divorce more common <u>among those in their 20's.</u>

Support 2: <u>Suicide</u> more common in <u>70's</u>

Support 3: Emotional stability study – distress <u>does not occur more often in midlife years</u>

Support 4: If crisis, not from age <u>but other events like divorce or illness</u>

5 Synthesizing Page 95
A

	Early Adulthood	Middle Adulthood
Physically	at a peak	*Declining*
Relationships	*Developing new relationships, establishing new family*	Settled as either single or married
Jobs	*exploring different directions starting out on career path*	Established and usually satisfied
Personal focus	on self	*On family and others*
Children	may have very young children	*Children are older, more independent and leaving home*
New responsibilities	*for family and job*	For aging parents

Reading 3 – Late Adulthood
After You Read

1 Comprehension after speed reading Pages 100–101
B

1. a   2. c   3. a   4. b   5. a
6. b   7. c   8. c   9. b   10. b

2 Describing change Pages 101–102
A

1. f   2. g   3. e   4. c
5. b   6. d   7. a

B

1. deteriorating
2. shrink
3. subside
4. diminishing
5. fade

Chapter 4 Academic Vocabulary Review

Page 104

1. shift
2. contradiction
3. perceive
4. emerge
5. attain
6. trigger
7. concept
8. presume
9. framework
10. attitude
11. stability
12. compensate

Chapter 5
Body Language

Reading 1 – Gestural Communication

Preparing to Read

Thinking about the topic Page 112

Answers may vary.

1. affect displays
2. regulators
3. emblems
4. adaptors
5. illustrators

After You Read

1 Outlining practice Page 116
A

I. Introduction
   A. Definition of non-verbal communication (NVC):
      Communication without words
   B. Reasons it is important to be able to use NVC
      effectively
      1. Higher attraction, popularity and psychosocial
         well-being
      2. More popular in many interpersonal
         communication situations
II. Types of Gesture
   A. Emblems
   B. Illustrators
   C. Affect displays
   D. Regulators
   E. Adaptors
      1. self-adaptors
      2. alter-adapters:
      3. object-adapters

2 Highlighting Pages 116–117
A

Students should highlight the following definitions:
emblems: body movements that have rather specific translations
affect displays: the movements of the facial area that convey emotional meaning
regulators: monitor, maintain, or control the speaking of another individual
illustrators: accompany and literally illustrate verbal messages

adaptors: unintentional movements that usually go unnoticed
self-adaptors: usually satisfy a physical need, generally serving to make you more comfortable
alter-adapters: body movements you make in response to your current interactions.
object-adaptors: movements that involve your manipulation of some object.

B

Students should highlight some of the following examples for each term.
emblems: "OK," "Peace," "Come here," "Go away," "Who me?," "Be quiet," "I'm warning you," "I'm tired," and "It's cold." Also, nothing and zero.
affect displays: expressions that show anger and fear, happiness and surprise, eagerness and fatigue
regulators: When you listen to another, you are not passive; you nod your head, purse your lips, adjust your eye focus, and make various paralinguistic sounds such as "mm-mm" or "tsk."
illustrators: In saying, "Let's go up," for example, you probably move your head and perhaps your finger in an upward direction. In describing a circle or a square, you more than likely make circular or square movements with your hands.
adaptors: self-adaptors: moistening lips, pushing hair
                  out of eyes
      alter-adaptors: crossing arms over chest,
                  moving closer to someone
                  you like
      object-adaptors: clicking a ballpoint pen,
                  chewing on a pencil

4 Defining language Page 118
B

illustrators, regulators, self-adaptors

C

Possible responses:

Illustrators are movements that accompany and literally illustrate verbal messages.

Regulators are body movements that monitor, maintain, or control the speaking of another individual.

Self-adaptors are the movements that satisfy a physical need.

5 Signaling examples Page 118

A

Possible responses:

such as, for example, examples include, are (movements) that involve

Reading 2 – Facial Communication

Preparing to Read

1 Skimming Page 120

a. Section 1
b. Section 2
c. Section 3
d. Section 2
e. Section 1

2 Words related to the topic Page 120

C

happy
afraid, fearful
sad
disgusted, disgusted
bewildered

surprised
angry
interested, interesting
contemptible, contemptuous
determined

After You Read

2 Guessing meaning from context Pages 124–125

Possible responses:

glum: not happy
vicious: not peaceful and friendly
frowning: an expression on the face that shows one is not happy
gloating: being very excited
violate: don't follow
insensitive: not caring, cruel

simulate: make
mimicking: making
subjects: people, participants

stands for: means
cataloged: identified,
last: stay, keep

Reading 3 – Eye Communication

Preparing to Read

1 Ways of looking Page 127

1. g   2. e   3. f   4. d   5. b   6. a   7. c

After You Read

1 Comprehension after speed reading Pages 131–132

B

1. c   6. a
2. b   7. c
3. b   8. c
4. b   9. a
5. c   10. b

Chapter 5 Academic Vocabulary Review

Page 134

1. mutual
2. series
3. maintain
4. consequently
5. arbitrary
6. exceed
7. signify
8. modify
9. hypothesis
10. conclusion
11. duration
12. interpret

Developing Writing Skills

Summarizing Pages 135–136

D

a. 4   b. 2   c. 5   d. 1   e. 6   f. 3   g. 7

E

Our facial expressions can express how we feel, hide how we feel, and even affect how we feel. Common facial expressions, such as happiness or fear, easily express how we feel and are fairly easy to interpret. We are also, however, capable of putting expressions on our face that deceive people and don't allow them to perceive what we are really feeling. Finally, according to the facial feedback hypothesis, it seems that simply adopting a certain facial expression can influence our emotional state.

F

Answers will vary.

Chapter 6
Touch, Space, and Culture

Reading 1 – The Meanings Of Touch

Preparing to Read

2 Skimming Page 137

Paragraph 1: haptics
Paragraph 2: intimates or those with a relatively close relationship
Paragraph 3: yes
Paragraph 4: behaviors, attitudes, feelings
Paragraph 5: during greetings or departures
Paragraph 6: removing a speck of dust from someone's face, or helping someone out of a car, or checking someone's forehead for a fever.
Paragraph 9: older people

After You Read

1 Reading for details Page 140
A

1. c   2. a   3. d   4. b   5. e

B

1. less than
2. more than
3. less than
4. more than
5. less than

2 The passive voice Pages 140–141
A

1. is touched by
2. touch
3. touches
4. be touched by
5. are touched by
6. touches
7. touch

3 Word families Pages 141–142
A

1. avoidance
2. disclosure
3. dominance
4. greetings
5. intimacy
6. playfulness
7. ritualistic
8. tips
9. variety

B

The amount of touching varies depending on the degree of intimacy between two people. Although in certain ritualistic situations, such as during a greeting, people who are not so intimate may touch by shaking hands. Research shows that certain people who don't like to disclose personal details about themselves try to avoid touching other people as much as possible. Touch avoidance also may occur as people get older.

Reading 2 – Spatial Messages

After You Read

1 Making a chart Page 146

	distance in close phase	distance in far phase	typical relationship between people	examples of what one can see or smell	Amount of eye contact or voice level used
intimate distance	**Actual touching**	**6-18 inches**	lovers	**Sound, smell, and feel of each others' breath**	**Eyes seldom meet**
personal distance	18 inches	**4 feet**	**Loved ones**	Breath odor	
social distance	**4 feet**	12 feet	**Business or social acquaintances**		More eye contact Louder voice
public distance	**12 feet**	**More than 25 feet**	dangerous-looking strangers public figures	**No facial details A whole setting, not separate individuals**	**No eye contact Exaggerated voice**

2 Using adverbs Page 147

A

1. In intimate distance
   In the close phase

2. In the close phase
   In the far phase

3. At the social distance
   At this distance
   In offices of high officials

4. In the close phase
   At this distance
   On a public bus or train
   At the far phase

C

1. evidently
5. clearly
7. unexpectedly
10. apparently
12. fortunately

3 Answering a short-answer test question Page 148

Answers will vary.

Reading 3 – Nonverbal Communication and Culture

Preparing to Read

1 Skimming Page 149

■ Cultural differences in spatial behavior
■ Cultural differences in eye contact
■ Cultural differences in touch behavior

After You Read

1 The passive voice Page 154

A

1. Folding your arms over your chest <u>would be considered</u> defiant and disrespectful in Fiji. Tapping your two index fingers together <u>would be considered</u> an invitation to sleep together in Egypt. Bowing to a lesser degree than your host <u>would be considered</u> a statement of your superiority in Japan.

Inserting your thumb between your index and middle finger in a clenched fist <u>would be viewed</u> as a wish that evil fall on the person in some African countries

2. emotions are facially expressed; it is considered,

3. were based on, are not served, is viewed, is to be avoided, it is considered, are socialized, can be interpreted, may be perceived, who may in turn be perceived

4. one: a bow is often required.

5. none

3 Transitional expressions Pages 155–156

A

For example, so, on the other hand, so

B

Paragraph 4: For example (E); but (C); Therefore (R),
Paragraph 6: For example (E); In contrast (C)
Paragraph 7: for example (E); however (C); consequently (R);
Paragraph 8: As a result (C); For example (E)

4 Collocations Page 156

A

1. broad smile
2. clenched fist
3. common gesture
4. direct eye contact
5. fundamental difference
6. neutral expression
7. risky undertaking
8. short period
9. well-documented finding
10. wide variation

Chapter 6 Academic Vocabulary Review

Page 158

1. detect
2. circumstances
3. sustain
4. restrictions
5. initiate
6. enable
7. reveal
8. emphasize
9. fundamental
10. correspond
11. visual
12. reluctant

Chapter 7
Friendship

Previewing the Unit

Chapter 7: Friendship Page 165
A

1. Yes 2. No 3. No 4. No 5. Yes

Reading 1 – What Is Friendship?

Preparing to Read

2 Predicting Page 166
A

1. d 2. b 3. e 4. a 5. c

After You Read

1 Using new words in context Page 171
A

Possible Answers:

1. wide array – a large number of something, each being different
2. mutual positive regard – both people like one another
3. voluntary – by one's own choosing
4. via – through the use of
5. prowess – above average skill or talent
6. guarded – closed off, defensive, shy
7. dispelling – proving to be untrue
8. hang out – be casual with another person

2 Outlining practice Page 172
A

I. A: Interpersonal relationship
    C: Mutual positive regard
II. B: Affirmation
    C. Ego Support
    D. Stimulation
III. A. Contact
     B. Involvement
     D. Dissolution

4 Understanding paragraph structure Page 173
A

1. Three parts
2. 2 and 3 define the term *interpersonal relationship*, 4 and 5 define the term *mutually productive*, and 6 and 7 define the term *mutual positive regard*.
3. Second and Third
4. It signals an additional piece of information.
5. They each help to explain the three terms which define friendship.

Reading 2 – The First Encounter

After You Read

1 Reading for details Page 178
A

1. NR	7. R
2. NR	8. NR
3. R	9. R
4. NR	10. NR
5. R	11. R
6. R	12. NR

Reading 3 – The Internet and Relationships

After You Read

1 Comprehension after speed reading Pages 183–184
B

1. a 2. c 3. b 4. c 5. a
6. b 7. a 8. c 9. a 10. a

2 Collocations Page 185

A

1. positive
2. offer
3. a cloak
4. provide, intimacy
5. tremendous
6. TV time
7. great

Chapter 7 Academic Vocabulary Review

Page 187

1. flexible
2. widespread
3. reassess
4. via
5. despite
6. assigned
7. concentrate
8. prospective
9. voluntary
10. aspect
11. expand
12. irrelevant

Developing Writing Skills

Pages 188–189

A

1. Italics
2. Only the first time she quotes it.
3. She uses his full name only the first time, and only his last name every other time.
4. **In** – start of sentence; **T**he **I**nterpersonal **C**ommunication **B**ook – title of book; **J**oseph **D**eVito – proper name; "**O**ne way…" – quote which is the start of a sentence; **F**or example… – new sentence; **A**ccording to… – new sentence; **O**ne of … – new sentence.
5. *Students should try to come up with the following rules*:

- Commas are used to separate a phrase that comes at the beginning of a sentence before the main subject and verb of the sentence:
    In The Interpersonal Communication Book,
    According to DeVito,
    For example,
- Commas are used to separate a transitional phrase in the middle of a sentence:
    friends, for example, is from…

- Commas are used to separate items in a list:
    previously unfamiliar people, issues, religions, cultures, and experiences
- A comma is used to separate a reporting verb from the direct speech that follows it:
    Joseph DeVito writes, "One way…"

6. *Students should try to come up with at least the following rules by analyzing this quotation*:
    Joseph DeVito writes, "One way… ."

- After the reporting verb and before the direct quotation, a comma separates the verb from the beginning of the quotation.
- Following the comma, beginning quotation marks are used: "…
- Following the beginning quotation marks the first letter of the first word is capitalized.
- At the end of the quotation, end of sentence punctuation is used – either a period, question mark, or an exclamation point.
- Outside the final punctuation, end quotation marks are used: … ."

Students should try to come up with two other rules by analyzing this other use of a quotation in the text:
    because this person could "help bring you into contact with previously unfamiliar people, issues, religions, cultures, and experiences."

- When no reporting verb is used and the quotation is used as part of a grammatical sentence, no comma is used before the beginning of the quotation and the first letter is not capitalized.

B

Some people find it very difficult to make friends or meet people. Perhaps they are shy or they live in a small town where there are not many opportunities to make friends. For such people, the Internet is ideal. As Weiten et al write, "[T]he Web offers a wealth of opportunities to interact for those normally separated because of geography, physical infirmity, or social anxiety." "Of course," as they also point out, "the anonymous nature of Internet communication does make it easy for dishonest individuals to take advantage of others…"

Chapter 8
Love

Reading 1 – Attraction Theory
After You Read

1 Reading for main ideas Page 193
Similarity
> One is very likely to find someone attractive if they look, act, and think very much like you.

Proximity
> People that you find attractive are likely to live or work close to you.

Reinforcement
> We often find attractive people who give rewards and reinforcements.

Physical Attractiveness and Personality
> People like people more when they are physically attractive and have a pleasant personality.

Socioeconomic and Educational Status
> Men are usually attracted to women with a lower socioeconomic status, but women find higher socioeconomic status more attractive.

2 Mnemonics Pages 193–194
A

2P R 2S
2P = [Physical Attractiveness and Personality] and [Proximity]
R = [Reinforcement]
2S = [Similarity] and [Socioeconomic and Educational Status]

B

SuPPeRS
S [Similarity]uP[Physical Attractiveness and Personality] P[Proximity]eR[Reinforcement]S[Socioeconomic and Educational Status]

C

Papa Says Porcupines Sometimes Run.
Papa [Physical Attractiveness and Personality] Says [Similarity] Porcupines [Proximity] Sometimes [Socioeconomic and Educational Status] Run [Reinforcement].

4 Prepositions Page 195
A
a. to
b. in
c. on
d. to
e. to
f. with
g. to
h. to
i. with
j. on

Reading 2 – Types of Love
Preparing to Read

Words related to the topic Page 196
1. a, j, n
2. l, h, d
3. g, o
4. c, i, k
5. f
6. b, e, m

After You Read

1 Reading for details Page 200
1. c   2. f   3. e   4. a   5. b   6. d

Reading 3 – Gender Differences in Loving
After You Read

1 Reading for details Page 205

	Men	Women
1.		x
2.		x
3.		x
4.	x	x
5.	x	x
6.	x	x
7.	x	
8.		x
9.	x	x
10.	x	

2 Similar and Different Pages 205–206

A

adjective	noun	verb	adverb
similar	similarity		similarly
different	difference	differ	differently

C

1. similar
2. different
3. difference
4. similarity
5. difference
6. differ
7. difference
8. differently
9. similarly
10. difference

3 The passive voice Pages 206–207

A

1. people in the United States
2. writers and the mass media
3. writers and the mass media
4. researchers
5. researchers
6. the reader, you

B

were surveyed; was revealed; was predicted; was found

Chapter 8 Academic Vocabulary Review

Page 208

1. unattainable
2. attributes
3. investigate
4. construct
5. unique
6. conception
7. exhibit
8. potential
9. compatibility
10. principle
11. consistent
12. justify

Unit 1 • Content Quiz

Part 1 True/False questions (24 points)

Decide if the following statements are true (T) or false (F).

_____ 1. Stressors are events or factors that cause stress.

_____ 2. No studies have found a link between continual stress and greater susceptibility to physical illness.

_____ 3. The leading cause of death in the United States is cancer.

_____ 4. A pattern of behavior, labeled Type A behavior, has been identified as that which many believe is more likely to lead to heart disease.

_____ 5. Despite all the health warnings, the number of smokers in the United States continues to rise each year.

_____ 6. There are many studies that have shown that depressed people who exercise regularly can reduce the amount of depression that they feel.

Part 2 Multiple choice questions (24 points)

Circle the best answer from the choices listed.

1. What do all stressful events have in common?

   a. They lead to suffering, illness, or pain

   b. They interfere with our everyday life or routine.

   c. They give rise to feelings of anger or fear

   d. They lead to alarm reaction, resistance, and collapse.

2. Which of the following would *not* be good advice to help an individual cope with a stressful event?

   a. Think of the stressful event as a danger or a threat.

   b. Try to predict what is going to happen.

   c. Gain some control over what is going to happen.

   d. Be realistic and understand that stressful events are unavoidable in life.

3. Which of the following would *not* be identified as a risk factor for heart disease for a Type B personality?

   a. a high cholesterol level

   b. smoking

   c. a family history of heart disease

   d. a stressful job

4. Which of the following has been used to try to explain why religiously active individuals tend to live longer than non-religious individuals?

   a. They tend to live alone.

   b. They tend to be women.

   c. They tend to exercise more.

   d. They tend to visit their doctors more frequently.

Part 3 Short answer questions (24 points)

Write a short answer to each of the following questions. In most cases no more than one or two sentences are required.

1. Describe two characteristics of people who are said to have "stress-resistant" personalities.

2. What are three differences between people who are said to have Type A personalities and those said to have Type B personalities.

3. Compare smoking trends in Canada and China.

Part 4 One paragraph or short essay answer (28 points)

Choose one of the following topics and write a paragraph or short essay about it.

1. Connections between the amount of stress in one's life and illness

2. A healthy lifestyle

Photocopiable

Unit 2 • Content Quiz

Part 1 True/False questions (24 points)

Decide if the following statements are true (T) or false (F).

_____ 1. Psychologists all agree that adolescence is a negative period of great turmoil and stress.

_____ 2. The growth spurt of early adolescence usually occurs in girls at an earlier age that it does in boys.

_____ 3. Adolescents tend to be great experimenters.

_____ 4. J.J. Arnett, who created the term "emerging adulthood," believes that *identity formation* usually comes to an end by one's late teens.

_____ 5. The "midlife crisis" is more stereotype than reality.

_____ 6. The percentage of those who say they fear death has been found to be highest amongst the most elderly.

Part 2 Multiple choice questions (24 points)

Circle the best answer from the choices listed.

1. Which of the following is *not* a characteristic of adolescent egocentrism?

   a. thinking other people are judging your appearance

   b. being very self-conscious

   c. thinking other people are talking about you

   d. trying to make people notice you as much as possible

2. Which of the following best describes the democratic parenting style?

   a. Parents act as friends and do not impose any rules or limits.

   b. Parents act as experts, give advice, and allow a certain degree of freedom, but do set limits.

   c. Parents are supportive, but interfere as little as possible in their children's lives.

   d. Parents are quite strict and are not willing to discuss any of the rules they impose on their children.

3. Which of the following would *not* typically be a question that a young adult would ask him or herself?

   a. Should I get married?

   b. What job should I get?

   c. How long should I wait before having children?

   d. What can I do to increase my chances of living a long and healthy life?

4. Which of the following is *not* one of the seven major challenges one must face in middle adulthood?

   a. adjusting to aging parents

   b. deciding what sort of career to devote one's life to

   c. achieving a sense of social and civic responsibility

   d. finding hobbies and interests to fill one's increased leisure time

Part 3 Short answer questions (24 points)

Write a short answer to each of the following questions. In most cases no more than one or two sentences are required.

1. What are the three ways of defining adolescence?

2. "Psychologically speaking, adulthood is marked by two possibilities that at first seem contradictory: (1) independence … [and] (2) interdependence." Explain this statement.

3. Define "emerging adulthood."

Part 4 One paragraph or short essay answer (28 points)

Choose one of the following topics and write a paragraph or short essay about it.

1. The problems and benefits associated with being an early or a late bloomer during adolescence

2. The myth of the "midlife crisis"

Unit 3 • Content Quiz

Part 1 True/False questions (24 points)

Decide if the following statements are true (T) or false (F).

_____ 1. Scratching one's nose when it itches is an example of an adaptor gesture.

_____ 2. Facial expressions appear to be different in different cultures.

_____ 3. We are more likely to judge a person positively if the person has dilated pupils.

_____ 4. In the United States, if people touch briefly during a task-related activity, such as giving change at a restaurant, the person touched is likely to have a negative opinion of the person who touches.

_____ 5. The closer you are to a stranger, the more likely you are to avoid eye contact.

_____ 6. Women tend to make longer eye contact than men, both when interacting with other women and with men.

Part 2 Multiple choice questions (24 points)

Circle the best answer from the choices listed.

1. The study of the way people gesture and use body movements is called _____ .

   a. haptics

   b. kinesics

   c. proxemics

   d. occulesis

2. When "reading" someone's facial expression, which of the following is most difficult to know.

   a. when someone is happy

   b. when someone is surprised

   c. when someone is lying

   d. when someone is feeling angry

3. Two coworkers are talking at an office party. What distance are they likely to keep between them?

   a. intimate

   b. personal

   c. social

   d. public

4. Long eye contact in Japan may often be received as a sign of _____ .

   a. lack of respect

   b. great honesty

   c. coldness

   d. great respect

Part 3 Short answer questions (24 points)

Write a short answer to each of the following questions. In most cases no more than one or two sentences are required.

1. Explain briefly the facial feedback hypothesis.

2. Name and describe two important functions of eye contact.

3. Define ritual touching and give examples.

Part 4 One paragraph or short essay answer (28 points)

Choose one of the following topics and write a paragraph or short essay about it.

1. Which appear to be more universal and why: facial expressions or gestures?

2. Important lessons in body language when interacting with people from different cultures

Unit 4 • Content Quiz

Part 1 True/False questions (24 points)

Decide if the following statements are true (T) or false (F).

_____ 1. Most friendships in the United States are voluntary relationships.

_____ 2. A good opening line when you see someone whom you would like to start a conversation with and get to know is "Haven't I seen you here before?"

_____ 3. Research shows that just under 50 percent of romantic relationships that start on the Internet lead to marriage or a permanent relationship two years later.

_____ 4. Men tend to prefer to have romantic relationships with women of lower socioeconomic and educational status than themselves.

_____ 5. The ludic lover is most interested in a long, peaceful, and satisfying relationship, similar to a friendship.

_____ 6. More women than men said they would marry someone they weren't in love with.

Part 2 Multiple choice questions (24 points)

Circle the best answer from the choices listed.

1. If a friend helps you find a new job, this is an example of his or her _____ value.

   a. stimulation

   b. ego-support

   c. affirmation

   d. utility

2. Which of the following nonverbal behaviors is *not* recommended on a first encounter?

   a. getting fairly close physically

   b. maintaining steady eye contact

   c. smiling

   d. sitting with arms folded across the chest

3. When two people who work in the same office become attracted to each other, which factor in Attraction Theory most likely explains this?

   a. reinforcement

   b. socioeconomic and educational status

   c. similarity

   d. proximity

4. Which type of lover is not focused on an individual, but on humanity as a whole?

   a. the manic lover

   b. the agapic lover

   c. the pragma lover

   d. the storgic lover

Part 3 Short answer questions (24 points)

Write a short answer to each of the following questions. In most cases no more than one or two sentences are required.

1. Describe three examples of recommended verbal behavior when trying to make a good impression on someone during a first encounter.

2. According to research, give one reason that some relationships that start on the Internet can be more successful than relationships that start as face-to-face encounters and one reason they can be less successful.

3. Define the *similarity principle* in Attraction Theory.

Part 4 One paragraph or short essay answer (28 points)

Choose one of the following topics and write a paragraph or short essay about it.

1. The four stages of friendship

2. Gender differences in loving

Photocopiable

Content Quiz Answer Keys

Unit 1

Part 1 True/False questions (24 points)
1. T   2. F   3. F   4. T   5. F   6. T

Part 2 Multiple choice questions (24 points)
1. b   2. a   3. d   4. b

Part 3 Short answer questions (24 points)
1. Stress-resistant personalities enjoy a challenge and like to feel control. When they do something, they are fully committed to doing it and not giving up.
2. Reference should be made to three of the following characteristics:
   Type A personalities are (1) more competitive, (2) more aggressive, (3) drive themselves harder, (4) are more likely to get into challenging situations, (5) are more intense, (6) have a greater sense of urgency than people with Type B personalities.
3. In the past 50 years, the number of smokers in Canada has decreased sharply; whereas in China, the number of smokers has soared. The number of female smokers in Canada is about equal to the number of male smokers, while in China ten times more men than women smoke.

Part 4 One paragraph or short essay answer (28 points)
1. A good piece of writing should explain what stressors are (they disrupt one's usual routine and way of life) and reference the Hans Seyle hypothesis that the more major the stressor, the more likely that one will become ill. Mention should also be made of research that shows that continual stress often makes the immune system weaker. Some typical illnesses that are associated with great stress should be mentioned, such as ulcers. The writer should probably note that a causal link between stress and cancer is not yet proven.
2. Many aspects of this unit may be drawn upon to write on this topic: coping with stress well by adopting certain behaviors that lessen the impact of the stressors; avoiding Type A personality behaviors, which seems to make individuals more prone to heart attacks; not smoking; exercising regularly; and eating a healthy low-fat diet. A really complete answer would speculate on why religiously active people live longer and are healthier. This could include belonging to a community, having a sense of purpose, and adopting a meditative approach to life.

Unit 2

Part 1 True/False questions (24 points)

1. F   2. T   3. T   4. F   5. T   6. F

Part 2 Multiple choice questions (24 points)

1. d   2. b   3. d   4. b

Part 3 Short answer questions (24 points)

1. Adolescence can be defined physically (how an individual's body changes), psychologically (how an individual's thought process, feelings, and behaviors change), and socially (how an individual's social status changes).
2. In adulthood, individuals learn to become independent of their parents; on the other hand, they develop new intimate relationships, with friends or a spouse, and have to learn how to live together with these people.
3. *Emerging adulthood* is a concept proposed by the developmental psychologist J. J. Arnett. It states that identity confusion, which is usually only associated with adolescence, is now occurring in young adults well into their twenties in developing countries. Emerging adults try to postpone the obligations of adulthood: a career, marriage, children, and home ownership as long as possible. They want to continue the experimentation that started in their adolescence into their twenties.

Part 4 One paragraph or short essay answer (28 points)

1. Reference should be made to self-esteem problems for late-blooming boys and the advantages for early-blooming girls and boys. A full answer should also mention that late-blooming girls are at a disadvantage during adolescence (in terms of self-esteem), but that this may turn out to be an advantage later in life, since they can concentrate better on studies and other interests.
2. In this answer, the writer should first describe the stereotypical behavior of a male in a midlife crisis, and of a woman. A well-balanced piece of writing might mention the physical decline that middle-aged people suffer through, which might explain why they should experience a crisis. However, the writer would then produce evidence that research shows less divorce, greater emotional stability, greater overall job satisfaction, less suicide, and more enjoyment of marriage in general amongst those in middle adulthood

Unit 3

Part 1 True/False questions (24 points)

1. T   2. F   3. T   4. F   5. T   6. F

Part 2 Multiple choice questions (24 points)

1. b   2. c   3. c   4. a

Part 3 Short answer questions (24 points)

1. The facial feedback hypothesis states that making a facial expression that shows a particular emotional state can actually lead to one feeling that emotional state. For example, if you make your face look like you are sad, you may start to feel sad.
2. Answers will include descriptions of two of the following functions: to monitor feedback, to secure attention, to regulate the conversation, to signal the nature of a relationship, to signal status, and to compensate for physical distance.
3. Ritual touching is most commonly defined as conventionally acceptable touching that takes place when people greet each other or depart from each other. The type of touching varies greatly depending on such factors as the gender, relationship, status, or culture of the participants.

Part 4 One paragraph or short essay answer (28 points)

1. The correct answer to this question is that facial expressions are more universal than gestures. There are generally accepted to be eight emotions that facial movements can communicate and that people asked to judge what emotion people are feeling can do so with fairly high degree of accuracy. It is also noted that although some cultures do not display the same facial expressions to the same degree, this is usually attributed to what is culturally permissible. The main evidence that gestures are not universal is the fact that "emblem" gestures vary widely from culture to culture.
2. A good answer to this question would touch on the need to understand cultural differences in body language when communicating with people from different cultures. Without this knowledge, misunderstanding can occur leading to failed communication. Gestures may be misinterpreted, as may different length of eye contact. The writer should also mention different expectations in touching behavior: some cultures are high contact cultures and some low.

Unit 4

Part 1 True/False questions (24 points)

1. T   2. F   3. F   4. T   5. F   6. T

Part 2 Multiple choice questions (24 points)

1. d   2. d   3. d   4. b

Part 3 Short answer questions (24 points)

1. The answer could include three of the following: Get the conversation focused on the person you are talking with; compliment the other person, but be sincere doing so; talk energetically; don't be too personal too quickly; find out what you have in common with the other person and talk about those things; and try to avoid yes/no questions.
2. One reason that relationships that start on the Internet can be more successful is that people feel more comfortable chatting when they are not face-to-face, so they build intimacy and rapport more quickly. One reason that they can be less successful is that people may reveal too many private details about themselves on the Internet, which can lead to an awkward or uncomfortable face-to-face meeting.
3. The similarity principle simply states that we tend to be attracted to and fall in love with people who are very much like ourselves; in other words, someone who looks like us, thinks like us, shares the same nationality, socioeconomic background, religion, and race.

Part 4 One paragraph or short essay answer (28 points)

1. In the answer to this question, reference must be made to the four stages that friendships can go through: contact, involvement, closeness and intimacy, and dissolution. Each stage should be described and examples given.
2. Reference should be made to research that shows that men tend to be more romantic about marriage than women, and less likely to cause a breakup by finding another partner. Men tend to believe in love at first sight more than women. Also girls tend to be infatuated and fall in love as teenagers at a slightly younger age than men.